USING THIS BOOK

*One of the best ways of helping children to learn to read is by reading stories to them and with them. This way they learn what **reading** is, and they will gradually come to recognise many words, and begin to read for themselves.*

First, grown-ups read the story on the left-hand pages aloud to the child.

You can reread the story as often as the child enjoys hearing it. Talk about the pictures as you go.

Later the child will read the words under the pictures on the right-hand page.

The pages at the back of the book will give you some ideas for helping your child to read.

British Library Cataloguing in Publication Data
McCullagh, Sheila K.
 Two green ears. — (Puddle Lane. Series no. 855. Stage 1; v. 8)
 1. Readers — 1950-
 I. Title   II. Rowe, Gavin   III. Series
 823'.914[J]   PZ7
 ISBN 0-7214-0915-6

First edition

Published by Ladybird Books Ltd Loughborough Leicestershire UK
Ladybird Books Inc Lewiston Maine 04240 USA

© Text and layout SHEILA McCULLAGH MCMLXXXV
© In publication LADYBIRD BOOKS LTD MCMLXXXV

Two green ears

written by SHEILA McCULLAGH
illustrated by GAVIN ROWE

This book belongs to:

Adrian

Lots of love from Gran

Ladybird Books

Christmas 1987.

Sarah lived in Puddle Lane.
She had a brother,
whose name was Davy.

Sarah

There was a big old house
at the end of the lane.
The house was empty.
It had a big garden.
Nobody minded if children played
in the garden.
One day, Sarah and Davy
went into the garden to play.

the old house

"I do wish the Griffle would
come back," said Davy.
"The Griffle is a monster,
and he sometimes comes to play with me.
He can vanish in bits.
Sometimes, you can only see his ears.
Sometimes, you can only see his eyes.
But I haven't seen him
for a long, long time."

"I wish he'd come now," said Sarah.

Sarah and Davy

But Sarah and Davy didn't see
the Griffle in the garden.
They went on playing by themselves.
They played by the gates,
but they didn't see the Griffle.

Sarah and Davy
didn't see the Griffle.

There was a big tree
in the garden.
Sarah and Davy played
in a big hole in the tree,
but they didn't see the Griffle.

Sarah and Davy
didn't see the Griffle.

Sarah and Davy played by the house,
but they didn't see the Griffle.

Sarah and Davy
didn't see the Griffle.

At last, it was time to go home.
Sarah and Davy
went out of the gates,
and down the lane.

"I **do** wish we'd seen the Griffle,"
said Sarah.

"So do I," said Davy.

Sarah and Davy
went out of the gates.

A dog lived in a house
at the other end of the lane.
He was a very big dog,
and he was very fierce.
Sarah and Davy liked most dogs,
but they didn't like this one.

the dog

As Sarah and Davy
went down the lane,
the dog ran out of the house.

He ran up the lane
towards them, barking loudly.

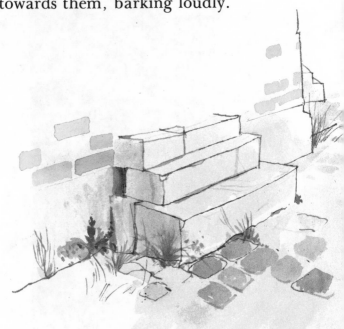

The dog ran
out of the house.

Sarah and Davy stopped.

They felt a bit frightened.
The big dog ran up to them,
barking.

The dog ran up
to Sarah and Davy.

Suddenly, the dog stopped.
He let out a howl.
His hair went up.
He looked up the lane,
past Sarah and Davy.

The dog looked
up the lane.

Sarah and Davy
turned round to look.

There was the Griffle!
The Griffle was standing
in the middle of the lane.
His eyes were very green,
and he was staring at the dog.

the dog
and the Griffle

The dog howled again.
He turned tail, and fled.
He ran away as fast as he could.
He ran back down the lane,
and into his house.

The dog ran away.

"Oh Griffle, I'm **so** glad
to see you," said Davy.
"I haven't seen you
for **such** a long time."

"**I've** seen **you**," said the Griffle.

"And now **I've** seen you too,"
said Sarah.

Sarah and Davy
and the Griffle

Sarah and Davy and the Griffle
went back to the gates.
They all went into the garden,
to play at hide and seek.

Sarah and Davy
and the Griffle
went back
to the gates.

Sarah and Davy hid first.
Sarah hid behind the tree.
Davy hid in the bushes.
But the Griffle soon found them.

Sarah and Davy

Then the Griffle hid.
The Griffle was very good at hiding.
But he always left his ears
or his tail showing,
so that Sarah and Davy
could see him.

The Griffle hid.

Notes for the parent/teacher

One of the most important things for children to learn, is that reading is something to **enjoy**. Make sure that both you and your child enjoy your 'reading times'. When you ask children to look and listen and read, be guided by what they feel they can and want to do. Let the child set the pace. A short session every day, or several times a week, is better than one long one.

When you have read the story, go back to the beginning. Look at each picture and talk about it, pointing to the caption below, and reading it aloud. Run your finger along under the words as you read, so that the child

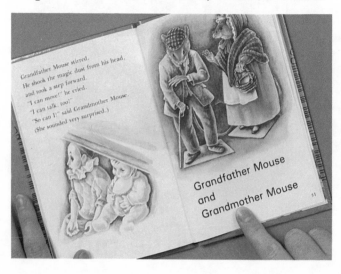

Grandfather Mouse stirred.
He shook the magic dust from his head,
and took a step forward.
"I can move!" he cried.
"I can talk, too!"
"So can I!" said Grandmother Mouse.
(She sounded very surprised.)

Grandfather Mouse and Grandmother Mouse

learns that reading goes from left to right. (You needn't say this. Children learn many useful things about reading by just reading with you. It is often better to let them learn by experience rather than by explanation.) When you come to page 5, talk about Sarah and then say, for example: 'Can you read this word?' (Suggestions about what you should say are just **suggestions**. Talking can become stilted if taken literally from a book so talk to the child in your own way.)

Continue through the whole book, looking at the illustrations and reading the captions. If a child doesn't know a word, tell her* what it is. If she can't read the caption on page 13, you might say: 'Did Sarah and Davy see the Griffle?' and if that doesn't help, then read the caption aloud. When you come to page 15, if the child still has difficulty, look back to page 13, and show her that the sentences on both pages are the same. Don't rush in with the word before she has time to think, but don't leave her floundering for too long. Encourage her to feel that she is successful; praise her when she does well and avoid criticism.

---

*Footnote: In order to avoid the continual "he or she", "him or her", the child is referred to in this book as "she". However, the stories are equally appropriate to boys and girls.

Now turn back to the beginning and print the child's name in the space on the title page, using ordinary, not capital letters. Let her watch you print it.

A child enjoys hearing the same story many times and the more opportunities she has of looking at the illustrations and **reading** the captions with you, the more she will come to recognise the words. Don't worry if she **remembers** rather than **reads** the captions. This is a normal stage in learning.

On the next three pages, there are words which the children have already met. Each word has a picture beside it. Ask the child to look at the pictures and read the words. Give her any help she needs. Then cover the pictures, and ask her to read the words again. As she reads each word, uncover the matching picture, so that she can check that she is right.

(Note: this is **not** a test. It is a way of encouraging the child to look at and to remember words. She should look at the pictures as often as she needs their help to read the words, and she should always feel successful.)

*Ask the child
to read the words,
first with the
pictures, and then
covering up the
pictures.*

Sarah

Davy

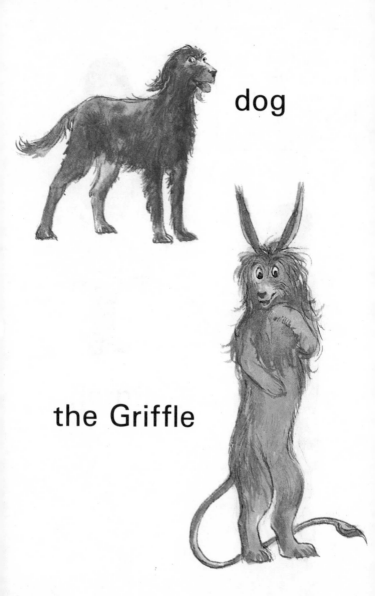

dog

the Griffle

gates

house

Puddle Lane Reading Programme   Stage 1

There are several books at this Stage about the same characters. All the books at each Stage are separate stories and are written at the same reading level.

The lists below show other titles available at Stages 1 and 2.

Stage 1

1 Tim Catchamouse
2 Tessa and the Magician
3 The magic box
4 Mrs Pitter-Patter and the Magician
5 The vanishing monster
6 The Wideawake Mice

Read the titles to the children.

the Wideawake Mice